Nectarines, Vodka, Sundays, and Death

poems by

Charles David James Case

Finishing Line Press
Georgetown, Kentucky

Nectarines, Vodka, Sundays, and Death

ACKNOWLEDGMENTS

"I Believe; The Goose, Mose Allison, and the Sky;" and "A Cat Door Speaks," first
appeared in *Beyond Bones,* III, D.H. Mayfair Publishing, 2011.

"Talking the City to Myself," first published in *Nomad,* Winter 2009.

"Afternoon Among Ruins," first published in *Nomad,* Summer 2011.

"Poetry Chores" and "Afternoon" first appeared in *A Celebration of Western New
York Poets,* Buffalo Legacy Publications, 2015.

"Watering Grass After Suicide," "Stage 4," "I remember walking across the dark
living room," and "February" first published in *Cholla Needles,* 6, 2017.

"The Sidewalk and the Fishbowl," first published in *Peach Mag,* October 2017.

"Moving Sideways in Four Parts," first published in *Ghost City Review,* November
2017.

Publisher: Leah Maines
Editor: Christen Kincaid
Cover Art: Charles David James Case
Author Photo: Amy Case
Cover Design: Elizabeth Maines McCleavy

Printed in the USA on acid-free paper.
Order online: www.finishinglinepress.com
also available on amazon.com

Author inquiries and mail orders:
Finishing Line Press
P. O. Box 1626
Georgetown, Kentucky 40324
U. S. A.

Table of Contents

Watering Grass After Suicide..1
Broken Plans 2
Poetry Chores 3
Stage 4 4
Red For Life..6
The Sidewalk And The Fishbowl 7
A Gentrified Neighborhood In Toronto...8
February...9
Atlanta...10
The Goose, Mose Allison, And The Sky 12
I Remember Walking Across The Dark Living Room.........................14
Sometime After Madison 16
I Believe 17
Karma Therapy 19
Afternoon 20
Saturday Afternoon, Little Italy...22
Red Eye 23
A Cat Door Speaks...24
Five Things I Want To Love More Than I Do 25
Map Of NY 27
A Christmas Conversation With Philip Freneau 28
Forty..31
First Poem To My Daughters..33
To My Youngest Daughter..35
Glimpses 36
Doctor...37
Tolerance 38
Chance 39
Impressions 40
Leader..41
The Condo Association's Oldest Ghost...42
Moving Sideways In Four Parts...43
Songwriter...45
Talking The City To Myself..46
Us...47
Purpose..48
The Zebra..49
We Bought A Chair For Mom To Die In...50

An Unwritten Postcard 52
Orange 53
Lunch 54
Afternoon Among Ruins 55
Winter 57
The Day And After 58
Confidential 59
Photosynthesis 60
Ingrid 61
We Met In Winter 62
Bargaining 63

To James and Florence,

You are on every page.

To Amy,

So much depends on you.

WATERING GRASS AFTER SUICIDE

The setting that carries farthest washes
the seed into the thick grass where
it will be choked off. So I pull the hose
and experiment with the nozzle, relearning
what I should already know. A gray squirrel
scratches at the corduroy bark of a nearby
maple. A deer breaks a branch somewhere
in the dark woods behind me. Then
it's noiseless again, calm like your marriage
to the outside world. For years, nobody
was sure if the beatings really stopped.
Now we're all left to piece together
private versions of your family life.
A few feet away where the ground
slopes down to the west, the water
has eroded channels that the weeds
will fill in if I don't. There I can see
the seed rise and clump for a moment,
quivering together in a tiny pool before
floating away, and I think of your sons
calling out for you as they opened a door
to find you hanging in the closet.

BROKEN PLANS

I spent the evening in a flood,
the trees lurching and stretching
in the storm. Inexperience
was innocence and innocence
the suburban palpitations
of the restless and dry.

Drowning was easy. A day slips,
a minute rises, and the remainder
falls away leaving no room
for juxtaposition. Duplication
becomes a function of wind
and rain.

I had met her while my wife
was out of town at a real estate
seminar. We had coffee and didn't
mean anything by it. But while I read
she looped her finger through mine
and smiled. I reached a hand

through the water. Without a control,
some light or heat, how could I
gauge the spoiling? This was
my baptism, my toothless heel
drowning in a matter of inches—easy
to feel changed.

It was a vagabond night
washed in a rain so complete my sins
must have floated away. There were no
alibis this time, no cubits. Its only salvation
was that it made desire
impractical.

POETRY CHORES

Allen Ginsberg never helped me do the laundry
as he talked away in long discourses,
pausing to breathe only at the end
of each thought. He made it exhausting
to separate the colors from the whites.
I tried to measure out a little less detergent
than I needed, so I could save some money,
and he questioned why I must be so clean.
Why must I wash my clothes for the capitalist swine herd?
Don't be a sheep to the hogs! He was incensed.
I resented his implication, but he stopped talking
long enough to watch me clean the dryer's rusty lint trap.

I have a howl of my own I tell him.
You will hear it when I take the dog out at night
and the rain drizzles along my shoulders stooped
forward in the dark. It's the sound of my hands
rustling in the pockets of my windbreaker,
that settled moment when I don't reach for your book,
and I cease wondering why I ache in the cold.
You have to listen carefully, but before I call the dog
to come in the house, I puncture the universe
with the gentle slide of my hands over nylon
so rebellious it refuses to let in the breeze.

I've toasted anarchy, too. I've rolled for days
in another's sweat and stale air as our half-crazed limbs
fought fatigue in between conversations about drugs
and liberation. I've allowed my words to go on and on
without end, and I have chastised everyone
who didn't listen. I love your poems, but
sometimes the dog jumps up on my pants
with muddy paws, and I am afraid that
in the daylight I won't be able to hide the stain.

STAGE 4

A bird I don't recognize barks
from the woods out back, its yawp beaten
down to a weary grunt by days of rain. It sounds
like it's struggling, maybe trying to drag
the moon through the oily night sky. I sit up in bed
to listen and my stomach spills onto my thighs
in the gray-blue haze, a lifeless blob on my lap
as useless as snake shed.

The bird stops and everything is still.
Not even the house creaks. I loved silence
once, when it was a sometime thing.
It's the world's way of speaking in tongues.
This morning, in the pre-dawn darkness, it says
a man lived here once. I wait for the bird
to lasso the fiery ball and drag it from hiding,
to lift the cold, humid bag that hangs

out of my skin. The noisy birds,
the guttural frogs, the lonely, sad erections
of old men. Nothing escapes. I imagine
the bird straining its neck, one end
of a frayed rope limp in its chipped beak,
the taut end tied to an impossibility.
It seems more real than the white bag dangling
from one side of my bloated abdomen.

The nurse said I looked good yesterday,
playfully adding that if she wasn't engaged . . .
She pulled back my blanket, her sun-browned
fingers brushing my emolliated skin,
grabbing the oozing, plastic sack with the sensual
indifference of repetition. An old idea
came to visit and won't leave. It's moved
in and we must die together.

She stopped wearing perfume last week.
Someone complained. A woman I bet,
or a man who went missing on himself.
I pretend to smell her over the prickly sting
of disinfectant that creeps across my eyes
with tiny legs. The idea stands up now,
running towards the yellow muck
trickling into the bag.

A man, a man still lives here. There it goes,
the present tense, down the stairs, busting
through the screen door, running across the yard,
inviting that damn bird to my funeral.

RED FOR LIFE

When the foxes mate, the cat
goes outside more often, sitting
at the edge of the woods, head
twitching, eyes resembling two
jaundiced, burlap circles glazed
with a predator's curiosity
as raspy squawks beat like the apple
of discord come to life under
some felled tree in the dark,
mucky acre next door where he
no longer hunts. One morning
he left a female cardinal's head
and wing by the back door. Torn
bits of down were glued inside
the maroon circle that had dried
overnight. Her red plume
was untouched and her still-glistening
eyes open as if she were waiting
for her mate. And where was he
I wondered? Sitting alone
in some tree, head swiveling
with a grub in his beak, waiting
to place it in her mouth with
a frenetic tenderness of little
stabs that she probably learned
to love years ago when they first
started together. Like a man
spilling red wine all over his wife
on their first date, it might
have been a funny story she told
to their children as their necks stretched
like nappy rubber bands and they
begged for more family history
they'd never hear.

THE SIDEWALK AND THE FISHBOWL

I have a confession. There is a sidewalk
under my tongue. I have two more confessions,
but they are inadvertent to the first, which
everyone knows, but nobody admits, is how
our lies pile up. My second confession
is that I see two of you. Each on top of the other.
God, that could be someone's fantasy. But
it's not like that anymore. The lines separating
you are clear. What I've made of you, and
what you are, like your confession that should
have come before mine, but instead came
as a secret from an apologetic friend who patted
my hand and waited for me to say a profound
word or two. But I just uttered a stupid "thank you"
as if someone had given me directions
to a museum with art I'd have to pretend
to understand. Sometimes I realize we live
in a fishbowl. I can hear the echo, tap
the glass. I run around the edge mouthing
silent questions to you, begging you
to tell me he didn't mean a thing. But
I can only hold my breath for so long,
and the sidewalk won't listen to reason.
So now all I do is sit here beneath
the castle and think of the two of you
entwined. I can't look away. I clutch
the image desperately, awestruck at how
unfamiliar my own house feels. But mostly
I look up and watch the bubbles rise
and bump off your skin until they slide
around you and float to the surface.

A GENTRIFIED NEIGHBORHOOD IN TORONTO

Her pants scuff with a washboard's rub
past the white-walled art cafés, tumbled book shops,
and second-hand smoke from better-than-usual
cigarettes. The street bustles with the rhythm
of a quickening pulse. Knit hats keep with changing
fashions instead of weather. A man reads the menu
to his boyfriend. An infant is swaddled to a young
mother's chest, his head floating from side to side.
Middle-aged men steady their breathing as they walk,
their shoulders stooped toward a different time.

The old woman wears a checkered head scarf
and sits with tattered and overflowing plastic bags
for a few minutes in each outdoor dining area
before rummaging the trash cans. She is speaking
some language to ease her shame. Maybe
she's saying, "See, this world is mine, too. We've dined
together," or, "I don't have to do this. It's my choice."
Ethiopian, Asian fusion, South Indian. Wherever she sits,
there is another country in the old woman's mouth
where she silently walks.

FEBRUARY

You were cold. Turning away
when you talked to yourself under the cloud
of cigarette smoke that hung just below
the ceiling. Flannel shirt untucked. Stooped
and mumbling your way into the next room.
You stared at the bird feeder for hours, your hand
jumping like a suffocating fish as you talked
to God knows what.

The winter sky always looked so close.
Once when I was six, wearing boots
with bread bags underneath to keep
my socks dry, I stood on the old fireplace
in the backyard and reached up like I
could grab the low, wax-paper clouds.

When I remember it now, sometimes
I'm seventeen and straddling those cobblestone
arms, still staring into the silhouetted
confessional of your pauper's Kabuki
theatre, your pageant of grief staged
in a drafty house. Life had become
an ethereal half shell of outsized dreams,
not quite life anymore, some middle ground
where we shoveled the driveway
but had no visitors.

I still see you, your trimmed beard
and shy brown eyes. Beige work coat.
Bright patches on the knees of your faded
jeans. One night in bed, when I had come
back for the weekend, your silence whispered
me your secrets, saying that if my dreams
can't destroy me, I haven't let them in.
They destroyed you, all crumbling
with that simple hope you'd grow
old with your wife.

ATLANTA

The security guard leans on a spongy elbow and mumbles
that it's a hub, and so I should expect such things as a retread
Burt Bacharach sloughing off a seersucker suit and a clean-shaven
Jesus complaining for the fifth time that he'd rather walk.

A young baggage handler confesses to Burt that he's given
too much away to the prying hands that always close in on him
like a brown and khaki prehensile jungle. He blames himself,
hanging his head as Jesus rips up his boarding pass, wounded

in obsolescence. Among those who travel light, only Hemingway
on his crutches, ashamed at his own relief, and
a smattering of reluctant business travelers, tired from walking
in place, look grateful for the moving pathway.

But the strangest thing is that Ubiquity introduces herself
to me as a proper noun. I shake her hand as I wait in line
for a sandwich and apologize for thinking her name
was Saturation. But, hell, what do I know? Everything

is everywhere at once: the trailing luggage, clouds
of bad cologne, coffee shop logos, beer taps, neon lights
on shoebox restaurants, fake wood, the smell of another
woman on my hands as I eat, my wife's voice

in the phone, our son's face in the lights. Nobody
is recognizable to me except the people who aren't
here. Jesus sleeps as security checks the bags of two
passengers waiting to board. I am traveling alone

once more. I fumble with the earrings I bought five
minutes ago and slip my ticket into the book
I'm not reading. The gangway is another planet with no
gravitational pull to hold me. As I sit the cabin air

is cool enough to peel away the therapeutic visions
I've superimposed on my life, and for a few moments

I can see the stewardesses and hear the meal cart's
stiff, ice-cube rattle. This is the cold,

delicate meaning of choices. Minor turbulence.
The pilot offers information. Jim Croce
fidgets next to me, his moustache damp
with a thin layer of someone else's sweat.

THE GOOSE, MOSE ALLISON, AND THE SKY

Friday morning. Mose Allison was on the radio
telling me about all sorts of things that are fine,
and things that once were fine, but aren't
anymore, like Mose Allison, and me. The goose
outside my car window, for his part, though overdressed,
was at ease. That goose was fine.

There is so much in a neck. It was bent down
alongside three deer, just one of the boys,
cool and well-placed, already drunk on Friday night.
They were all arches
eating from the same pile next to a footpath
off the highway, looking the same, except
that one came ready for the weekend,
dressed black tie for a khaki party.

I heard Mose say Friday nights
are a liberty emptying
by degrees, jumping wildly
among the lights until evening is all that is left. Liberty,
he went on, is a gardener planting the seeds
to its own demise.

As a child, I didn't have jazz, or Fridays.
I had brothers, deer, fields, and geese. I had the lonely
sky and demure tones. Tonight, I'll pray to the sky
because it's above me and I can know it.

I'll pray to Mose, too, because he's funky
with a strange cadence, and because he taught me
about Friday. Saturday morning I'll kneel
with the deer, and we'll pray to our brother
when he spreads his wings to carry himself
to another family where he looks and sounds
just a bit different, but never more fine.

There is so much in a neck. Just ask
the goose. But don't ask Mose; his voice
doesn't come from his neck. It comes
from someplace higher where
it cozies up to his heart and brain
to form a cool and impeccable trinity
that runs thick in the spaces
between consonants.

And don't ask me. I can't write
the way Mose could sing.

I REMEMBER WALKING ACROSS THE DARK LIVING ROOM

when I came home late and the only lights
were the small one over the kitchen sink
and the dim floor lamp next to your chair,
shrouding you in a yellow glow.
You sat alone, struggling to breathe, praying
that whatever sin caused your cancer
would be punished enough by your hair falling out
and lymphedema turning your skin purple
in front of your children.

Nobody yelled at me anymore
for coming home late. Instead, you asked me
for water and your lip balm, pointing
your small, quivering chin to the ceiling
so that gravity could help you swallow the few drops
that did not drib and fall down your neck.
I picked up your brush, careful not to bounce it
along your scalp, or pull out the few remaining wisps
as your lower lip trembled and your eyes
pooled in the light.

I forgot what I came to say, my tongue pinned
beneath your frailty. You looked up and told me
that men could cry. It was not until you called me your rock
as I came to say goodnight, and you reached
a withered hand that kept its white,
even against the yellow, that I realized
you were going to die.

At your funeral,
Sister Mary thought she was being kind,
telling me God picked you for his garden.
He only picks the prettiest flowers, she said.
I crossed myself; my face made no expression.
She was small and had dark, curly hair
like you had.
The night before, in the funeral home,

the showing room was dimly lit
and there was a lamp next to your casket,
again. Everyone said what a nice job they did.
But your lipstick was uneven, and your wig
not right. It was just something people said
when nothing else crossed their minds.
Nobody remarked that the green dress
they used to cover your purple was a cruel joke.

I never cried, never really cried,
for twenty years. But I stopped crossing myself,
really crossing myself, as I walked across
the cemetery grass that morning, the May sun
on my shoulder, to some stranger's car
that we used for show to go back home.

SOMETIME AFTER MADISON

Otis Redding died on December 10, 1967 when his plane crashed in Lake Monona near Madison, Wisconsin.

I'm sitting next to Otis Redding, our feet dangling
in the water. It's late summer. The evenings
are cool and we miss those muggy nights
when our skin was sticky just from sitting still.
Otis tells me he now understands how poets feel,
how they see their solitude walking next to them
like an out-of-body experience, and how they can't tell
the shadow from the object when they try to explain
what is always following them.

Ghosts disguised as whooping cranes glide
along the shore in the camouflage sunset. The breeze rises
and falls. I say I've gotten to know every person
I've lost by seeing the bookends of their lives without
getting hung up on my own vision
and unmet needs.

That's just how it goes, says Otis. Death
is the last time you get reintroduced
to the living, the final chance to shake hands
with a life.

I watch as a small stone he had been holding
all afternoon skips across the water. He
muses that the lifts and dives are the verses,
the shaky touch and go off the water
the refrains, the ripples the fade out.

Death is a funny time, he says. The whole world
is in bed and you're awake, waiting to put a bridge
between yourself and just one other person
who understands that the shadows
don't need the living.

I BELIEVE

I believe paperclips are the ballerinas
of the fastener world
the way they lock arms when they are together
and pirouette across my desk when they are free.

I believe the maple seeds falling
like helicopter blades in the park
expand the worlds of the lovers they dance around,
from their pressed palms to the treetops.

I believe matchsticks are foolish
for stalking the sun, but that they do it all the time, anyway,
believing they will burn brighter
in that brief moment when they get too close,
instead of being consumed.

I believe paper plates are altars
where young children can find their mothers' hands
giving them a hotdog and fresh ear of corn
dripping in butter at a summer picnic with the grass waving
like emerald streamers around them.

I believe skin wears better than cotton,
bodies belong together, cleanliness is overrated,
perfume is derelict, and the soft slip of fingers down a forearm
is God's handwriting.

I believe stripping naked at midnight
and reciting poems in my backyard
is prayer.

I believe a woman's voice is her heart
and would bottle the most melodic if I could
and drink them down like wine
while watching the sunset over the lake
as the waves gently slap the rocks below.
I believe youth and experience will stand trial together

wearing lampshades and giggling wildly
while those that are serious about marking time
look on in condemnation.

I believe music can harvest grain,
slop pigs, run a freight, win wars,
and mend all manner of wound.

I believe Shakespeare is finer than any shrink;
that a poem is its own audience; and that mothers, lovers,
matches, music, maple seeds, and ballerinas
can kindle a fire to light an entire life,
if we have even the smallest fragment
of combustible stuff within.

KARMA THERAPY

My mother turned one
on the day we dropped the first bomb,
a baby herself.

She inched three days
towards two when
Fat Man, twice as wide
as Little Boy, scorched
the island nation.

My brother said she cried
watching the planes carrying
the bodies of the boys of Vietnam
on the nightly news.

She would have wept
for the babies of Hiroshima
and Nagasaki, too.

She was a poor courier
for our Karma forty-some years
later, absorbing that radiation
as a cure.

I held her hand in the hospital
courtyard as she walked on a bench, still
believing, still smiling.

She told me the radiation burned
right through to her back.

AFTERNOON

I leaned my ladder against the window ledge
and watched afternoon undress. I felt strong
watching her bare skin, and the hair shaking
between her legs brought me peace of mind.

The curve
where her back led into her waist
revealed that each preceding day
led to this moment.

As a child I had looked out the window
on rainy afternoons,
watching the water pool and flood
the road in front of our house.

I imagined the rain would walk
into our living room and, looking confused,
ask me to play. I pretended it was not as vile
as my parents said to get caught in the rain.

But when it came, it came
with chaos and my father's shaking fist.
One day, the village came, too
and fixed that road.

I have seen days collapse
under their own weight causing time to disappear
without the universe
ever making up the difference.

I have seen days dressed in black,
and listened as their funeral hymns
trailed into endless silence.
Like the day they finished the road.

Morning split in two, its halves
held together with a few strands

of tissue that looked like threads;
there was a little blood.

Its jagged edges spread apart,
and she was born into the world
where I saw afternoon for the first time.
Her left hand emerged first

from the void, then the other.
She felt the house's uneven edges
as she pulled herself
from the entrails and bile.

She moved slowly, but when she
realized that everyone else
was overdressed, she leapt and twirled
about the room, slender and bare.

It was nearly two o'clock, and I
was working at something so important
that I barely noticed my inexperience
walking backwards into obscurity.

I barely noticed the naked afternoon
dancing as if no one could see.
I still look in on her when I need to pretend
that the out of place is blameless.

I never knew what was so important
that the village had to spend all that money.
But I know there is nothing like naked
to shake ambivalence off. And so

I miss that impossible flood out front,
but I remember the clinging smell of rain,
and the ends of her hair shaking around me
as the sun cascaded through the window.

SATURDAY AFTERNOON, LITTLE ITALY

Italian café,
the sun is out.
Fettuccini, plum tomatoes,
aglianico,
and an old book of poems
with a cover as chipped and shadowy
as the awning
beneath which I sit.

RED EYE

I didn't give much thought to the old lady
with the boy's haircut who kept asking
"What next?" until I was at my gate.

I told her to remove her coat.

"Do I still have to remove my shoes?" I said yes.

"What is that?" I explained the clear bag.

And after watching me a moment: "Now why are you doing that?"

I didn't answer. I simply felt small and so a few extra precautions
seemed a sort of offering.

Despite my ritual of reminding myself to stay awake,
I ran a red light on the way to the airport. The horns
were awful, like the warning shots of an angry god. And now
that I'm here, how am I to describe this place? As the belly
where our sunlight comes to die? The iridescent glow traces
a fingernail down my neck—a seduction, or
a school-yard prank.

I search for the old lady. She would be worried
for the crying babies, fidgeting, wanting to help.
Her old-world instincts creeping up, poking
their head out of the hole into the terminal,
frightened by the void.

I wish I could hear her tiny, porcelain voice
asking why the departure signs change so slowly,
or why the trash cans are bioluminescent.

It's the angry god, I can hear myself explaining,
pointing from the trash cans to the cameras, *watching*
to make sure we don't stop to sleep.

A CAT DOOR SPEAKS

A cat door speaks of many things,
the smallest of which
is the presence of a cat.

A cat door in a slave house
            speaks more.
A broken pipe fragment
or castor oil bottle,
with an old man's story
of his grandparents
keeping a small cabin
where they ate rations
and berries
is a miracle in the midst of injustice
at which we shake our heads

as if we could really begin to understand
that a cat door speaks of many things.

FIVE THINGS I WANT TO LOVE MORE THAN I DO

First, the rain. We've had so much this year, deluged
by a holdover from cheesy love songs and unoriginal clouds.
Just writing the word brings me to the jagged cliff
between self-reproach and unwelcome comfort.
I pumped out the basement six times in April.
Dear God, save me from easy metaphors.

Speaking of God, prayer. I always introduce myself,
like I have to shake God's hand before we can start. I apologize
for being a bother, a strange prelude from someone
who thinks himself worthy of a one-sided conversation
with the Almighty. Afterwards, I can't escape the fear
I was talking to myself.

Third, poetry. The end is the best moment, when
you wear the poem like a cobblestone coat that bruises
your ankles. You can't move without being reminded
your heart won't push enough blood to keep you upright.
But the feeling vaporizes under the smallest distraction—
misplaced keys, a child's cry. I feel like apologizing
to the poet. It's too much like prayer.

Fourth, this poem. I want lentil soup. If I go shopping
now and soak the lentils ahead of time, I can be done
by 2:00 and write until dinner. But that's not what will happen.
I'll dawdle searching for perfect soup music. Maybe
John Coltrane or Carla Bley. Then I will read,
find a great sentence, and go for a walk where
I will leave my best ideas in the Ramirez's flowerbed
on the corner. I have started and stopped myself from getting up
at least a dozen times the past thirty minutes.
I made my shopping list before writing number three.
Nina Simone: lentils spiced with cumin and revelation.

Last, my parents. This is true only if the conversation
I always have with them in my mirror is an insult
to their sacrifices. I fear so strongly it is that the reality

has grown irrelevant. I still can't let go of the things I embraced
over them when I was young, how I stubbornly confused
the temporary with the permanent. I hope they know
that my focus on aesthetics is waning. So much so
that I have changed my word for it. I used to call it art,
a word I now reserve for struggle.

MAP OF NY

In a cheap hotel bathed in exhaust
above 25th and 3rd you were the map
I unfolded, knowing that love is a matter
of geography, never the weather. I ran
my finger along your edges, felt the cracks.
Boot heels echoed past the door.

The gentle rustles and snaps as I
unfolded you. The humidity of the paper.
That slight must that rose to say you were
anxious, too. I bowed before the compass rose,
that scapegoat for unfinished journeys,
and traveled miles before we left the room.

A CHRISTMAS CONVERSATION
WITH PHILIP FRENEAU

Philip Freneau (1752-1832) was the poet of the American Revolution, a political satirist, ally of Thomas Jefferson, nationalist, and critic of John Adams. He froze to death at age 80 in a snowstorm, a week before Christmas, while walking home from a tavern.

Philip, did I tell you it was my feet moving
the ground yesterday? That thoughts of ending
our little experiment bled through my socks
and poured out the stitching of my dress shoes?

That I panted between the hungry skyscrapers
like a ravenous crow scavenging for the scraps
falling from the bank windows? That my heels
unleashed tremors and treason along the river

where our mermaids swim beneath unused grain
elevators, splashing their tails on the river ice
to seduce soft-boiled, pocket seditions from
the slender slip of the dreams that we have forgotten

in the march to prosperity? Of course not.
We've discussed so little, you and I. You are
as unreal as Grendel these days. With your
hooded eyes and French nose you're almost

Vaudevillian. Why won't you speak? You've
not toasted me once, Philip. My glass carries
nothing but honesty as I see it. You look away
and regard me as insane, or worse, spoiled

on your sacrifices. Perhaps you are sad
that you have to wait 'til spring for the mermaids
to pull themselves on the banks to whisper to you
in a language you made just for them? I'll tell you

a secret, Philip. Those young bodies won't be young
forever. The price tag is still on their tails,
and when you are away they mock you
to young men in sweater vests.

I see the judgment in your eyes, Philip.
You question what I know of sedition and seduction.
I know how to hold beauty, how to capture a moment
without the contraptions we've invented.

I know that the bartender measures our lives
against the snow. I know, too, that his is
a temporary salvation. But to be divine, just for
a moment, Philip, is still to touch the face of God.

I raise my glass to now, to life and beauty,
to having no revolution tonight, except our pens.
Look, at the end of the bar sit women with bare
shoulders dressed in naked immediacy.

Let's leave our heads and write lines between
their fingers and toes. Let's close our eyes
and ask them to guess which poems we are
imagining just by tracing their hands

along our palms. But if you insist on leaving,
Philip, I will follow. Together
we'll punctuate our paths until our forms
disappear in the storm.

One more for the road, brother.
The Footman leaves no prints.
Better the season to claim us
than an un-tabled sea of troubles.

Our histories will grow short, we will
soften, lie down in the snow, lose ourselves

in an ellipsis, and arrive home where we
are nothing more than our unfinished works.

FORTY

Last night in bed my wife said salt
and pepper. Then distinguished. I heard
my double is growing into me.
That man who started as a shadow

a few years back, quietly creeping
around the backseat of my car
while I searched for the news, some
sneaky little prick with my cleft chin.

On my back deck under the silver moon
I read one of those glossy news magazines.
It says we don't just taste salt
on the corners and edges of the tongue,

like they used to teach in school.
Same goes for sour, sweet, and the rest.
My dad and granddad before him
used to go to the front porch,

can of beer in hand, for a breath
of night air. But now we've left
our porches to enable our private myths,
uncomfortable in a world where taste

is hard to pin down. Maybe it's my age, or
the advertisement on page 62, but I have
this blind faith I can negotiate the twin riddles
of aging doppelgangers and masculinity

if I drink enough wine at the perfect hour
when the kitchen light behind me
makes the lonely, half-full,
maroon globe look like the sun

peeking over a silhouette of the earth
from outer space. The wine has a thousand

straws. I let a mouthful suck out
all the moisture until my tongue

feels like wool. Is it the umami,
or the bitter? Either way,
my research confirms
it's everywhere at once.

My double agrees
as the shadow and subject
become increasingly difficult
to tell apart.

Each sip is a prophecy,
a tiny piece of that silvery,
salty moon
hanging over my children.

FIRST POEM TO MY DAUGHTERS

Our room is orange and red. Meals
on yellow trays. Drinks in foil.
Thermostat at a decadent 75. The world
never so small or impossibly complicated

as swaddle blankets and take-out menus
on no sleep. You were born on a warm
October night that crept in after a clear
October day—the sky deep and long.

Leaves still shaking and changing
on the limbs below. I hope you're not
disappointed, but on day two of your
lives, I am wondering all about me.

I'm surprised, too. I might think of life,
how it begins, where it goes. Who you
will be. I could think about the different
textures of the diapers and blankets

and how those different textures might
foreshadow the differences in your two
paths. But it's about me. Whether
my procrastination is proof I am selfish

and lazy. Whether my writing means
I am only interested in my own
impressions. Or if my inability to focus
on one thing for too long will cause me

to miss something that will never come
again. Whether I am as inflexible
in matters of the heart
as I always have prided myself, and how

that will be good and bad for you.
My two dark-eyed daughters,

with your mysteries swaddled into the fabric
of your just-begun lives, you are

the new way life tastes like the sunlight
and changing leaves. The new immediacy
that makes cheap plastic straws
and Styrofoam feel organic and reborn.

The nurses take you three times a day
for more tests. Nine months ago, not here.
Yesterday, in your mother's belly.
Today, warm against my skin, even when

—especially when—you're not in the room.
Your mother's pale, tired fingers peel
the foil from cranberry juice as I sip
coffee I bought in the first-floor lobby.

Colostrum. Prolactin. Meconium.
Bilirubin. Quixotic dreams and short
attention spans aside, I remember
all the new words they tell me.

TO MY YOUNGEST DAUGHTER

I was eating breakfast, sitting in your oldest sister's chair,
so that I finally could have a seat at the head of the table,
when you cried that helpless cry I've learned to recognize.
You were scared, only one step away from me, wailing
with eyes closed and your face red, dangling
with your arm stuck through the slats of a dinner chair.

From the speakers next to the toaster, a slow clarinet
from the Maria Schneider Orchestra played the music
she'd written to one of my favorite Ted Kooser poems.
You rested your head on my left shoulder,
and a moment later, after a tremble and a descending whimper,
you were calm. Father and daughter swayed side to side,
heads touching on the dance floor of the kitchen.

You stayed like that for your entire childhood.
I watched you in the park. You must have been three or four,
your cheeks plump and splotchy from running
as you showed me how you balance on a big rock.
Then the yellow bus creaked to a stop in front of our house,
and I watched my last daughter take her first steps
away from me and her mom. A few years later,
you dropped your school project, which you had stayed up late
to finish, in the rain.

As you posed for a photograph, holding your diploma,
your gown hid that one-year-old who had got stuck
so easily, and you lifted your head up and smiled at me
on your way to my other shoulder. Not ten seconds later,
still in the kitchen, still swaying in the angled morning light,
during the father-daughter dance at your wedding,
you arched your back away, asking to go, just as I
was remembering this moment. You didn't see that my eyes
were watery. I hid them just so you wouldn't think twice
about turning away.

GLIMPSES

of the past trickle down
my frying pan and wash away
in a spiral down the sink.
Sun beams in parrot colors
petition loudly. It's morning
and I'm horny, but all I have
is garlic toast and coffee.
Not long ago someone else
used the frying pan and I
washed bacon grease and eggs
with diced shallots, sundried tomatoes,
and aged cheeses from it until
they swirled around the sink
and disappeared like sofas
or fine china sucked
into a plunging vortex
of irreconcilable differences
and smug lawyer looks.
This morning,
I wash off the dust.

DOCTOR

These things
happen.
Really.
All the time.

Nothing.
You worry.
That, too, is.
But don't.

Occasion
is only
a function
of here and there.

Pause, breathe,
count to ten.
Inhale, one.
Exhale two.

Balance
Balance
Balance

Think
of a window without glass
and a place that made you happy once.
Breathe.

Carry on
until the end.

Three minutes
short again.

TOLERANCE

when you narrow life
down to the bare essentials
you finally can afford intoxication

that moment when you forget
the mirror was your friend for those years
when your changes were imperceptible

CHANCE

no wonder why
it never came
a certain yesterday
in the shade trees
of stillborn buds
the serene, leafy wager

winless success
over/repeat again
no wonder why
it never came
a lost bet
a wanderer

but no revelation

IMPRESSIONS

Is there anything
left to be
discovered?

The moment passed
before
I captured it.

Maybe
ifIwritelikethisI'llfindrevelation.
But I don't.

Fleeting.
They all are.
Everyone says so.

LEADER

Celebration was premature.
Everybody understood
it's an outward thing, a
representation that other things
are in their place, not just any place.
Ascendancy exists
for its own sake. They didn't say it
that way, of course.

Everyone hid behind contempt
for common enemies and cigar smoke
drifted over the rolled-up sleeves
and hairy knuckles. Admitting
such things diminishes
the euphoria. Nobody said
what they were thinking.
So thinking stopped.

THE CONDO ASSOCIATION'S OLDEST GHOST

I can't tell you why there is a badger making me breakfast
anymore than I can explain why whenever I stub my elbow
my shoes don't fit for three days. I get as confused
as anyone when the rain stops by in an old nightgown
stroking her beard in the September morning asking me
for a cup of sugar and the phone book. I mean really,
who still uses a phone book these days?

But this is how the morning unfolds when the sun rises
in the west. I dare anyone to live under these circumstances,
what with the paint flaking itself off and dancing with my stockings,
the shag carpet taking a shower after the five a.m. news, and
my oven mitts playing poker and demanding more liquor
to pass the day. Who can keep up with it all?

Water into wine sounds great in scripture, but I found out
the hard way if you combine them in a glass at a party, everyone
just laughs at you. I have not been around long, but I can tell
humility is not a virtue. It leads to nothing but a concern about
place. It leads to faint praise, but no correction. This revelation
won't exorcise my trepidation. It won't magically lift my feet
one after the other to the angry sidewalk outside. The unreal
has always been too real. It's a wily animal that keeps coming
until you stop looking its way.

If I stand before the mirror, shaking my fist at time
like a flowerless, craggy hibiscus branch, what would I really have
on the girl in the next apartment wearing nothing but a bright-orange
necklace with a distant look in her eye? For my part I just wonder
if her bedroom really smells like Paraguay in late spring.
I wonder if she really exists.

A man outside my window is walking down Delaware Avenue
with a Burmese python around his neck. He knows more
than me, but I can't figure out how.

MOVING SIDEWAYS IN FOUR PARTS

I. I Loved You When

We will find lovers for our improved
selves, that person the other had
wanted us to be. But nobody
will love the old us again.

II. Missing

I like to be hungry
on vacation. I go through too much
of my life well fed.

III. Sleep, Sex, and Poetry

Repetition doesn't matter.

The fact that I've done each
for decades is no assurance
I can do them again.

The past is no guide to the future.

Tiny differences in approach
can be disaster.

Anxiety is prophecy.

IV. Door

This is no
ordinary
metaphor.

I just saw it
for the first time.
This is no invitation.

In the streetlight
it's always there,
hiding in plain sight.

Stainless steel
and dirty glass.

A girl acts naturally.
This is no invitation.

SONGWRITER

stand on the corner beneath
the saffron streetlight umbrella

in the gulf night
and tourist cologne

recite my heart
for me

so I can pretend
everyone hears

TALKING THE CITY TO MYSELF

Sometimes while walking the city,
you get stuck in the rain.
You have to be careful stepping
the old sidewalks that look of shale
as you frenzy your pace to find shelter
from the harmless drops of water.

But promise me this: between your brown hair
that as caution grows into you,
you will forever remember
that the rain is only rain,
the cold only cold, and the glassy slate
is a blessing spread before you.

US

Convenience
is the
expectation.

Happiness
we measure by a ruler
whispering in our ear.

Love
we see
in the mirror.

Hate
much
the same,

our parents
standing
behind us

either way.

PURPOSE

I write for you.
Terrifying, isn't it?

Don't read too much
into that first line,
and don't go away.

Close your eyes, then
open them. Cover
those first four words.

They exist, under
your hand.

THE ZEBRA

My stripes are meant to be a liberty, to hide
me in plain sight among the heat waves
that rise from the Serengeti where
I once looked like the bending air

in the scorching sun. Now I'm a caged study
in contrasts for people throwing darts
at balloons for a sandwich bag
of erasers shaped like cows.

Sisyphus at least got to move. Tantalus
served his damnation outside. Tiresias
was spared the face paint and cotton candy.
But here I am, Prometheus

in prison stripes, shuffled from one
corrugated-metal-building town to the next.
My white now resembling the muddy snow
along the highway to the children's fair

where I stand on concrete for two days
surrounded by strollers and lights
that blink like a sea of impossibly
thoughtless eyes.

WE BOUGHT A CHAIR FOR MOM TO DIE IN

Maybe the cat's slow death was its punishment
for making Mom cry. It died the same way she did:
immobile, turning frail and withering from the inside.
Its own body betrayed it.

It's hard to blame it for being scared. She no longer
looked like herself. Her long hair, once permed
into mounds on her head, was gone. Half her torso
had turned the ghostly pale of death. The other half
was turning purple because her lymph nodes had been
harvested. The air around her stopped changing,
so she didn't even smell like herself.

The chair was new. The commode and strangers
moving in and out of the house were new. Umbilical
fluid and ice cream were replaced by a helpless
homeopathic healer and some nonsense
about her wounded inner child.

The animal bristled, yellow eyes bulging as its body
danced that wild, jerking dance that only a scared cat
can dance as it tried to get away.

The day she died, I had a tennis match. I didn't see
her. I don't remember if I won. I remember
that whatever happened, I was to keep being a kid.
I also remember two days before when the ambulance
arrived and people I had never seen before lifted her
from the chair to a gurney. I was told the chair was
for her comfort. I was not told about the ambulance, at all.

Her first death was easy. There was nothing to be done
except to watch and wait. Her second death, the time
we killed her, was much harder. A few feet of earth
is not nearly as heavy as the silence we piled on her life.
Cancer works quicker than forgetting.

Still we kept the chair.

There are few things I regret. Beating
the cat for being scared of Mom is one. So is
not taking a hunting knife to that chair.

AN UNWRITTEN POSTCARD

It's raining in the northeast where you are alone and tired in a forsaken, canal town with plywood windows and dangling gutters that occasionally slap the remaining shards of glass from a broken window below.

From a screened-in patio I watch a tanned woman around your age at the resort pool straighten an enormous towel under a blue umbrella.

Maybe she knows another 74-year-old widower with squamous cell who isn't a candidate for surgery.

Or maybe it was her who couldn't move out of her home after her spouse died, allowing a quarter-acre lot to become a cage decorated with a marble bird bath that had once been a baptismal font.

Or maybe her life has always been a pool, a small, respiring organ in the middle of an Orlando resort where her energy is replenished. That is until one day something crawls in the water, a Florida gator or maybe a deadly snake whose venom spreads before anyone knows it's there.

On the other side of the glass, in a room of stucco walls, your daughter-in-law, who still has that provocative, northeast pale to her skin, is wrestling sunscreen onto your granddaughters as they squirm and twist. Seconds ago, before I listened to your message, this had made me smile.

ORANGE

Orange is a three-syllable word masquerading as two. But its layers are at least
as deep as three, as deep as three and maybe more, which is why you should stop
and think about the way your mouth rolls over the break. It's a trickster,
a seductive thief gathering attention to itself as it gently reclines on the bed.
I thought it was an awakening. So I told myself I had been asleep. But
it was just a series of circles drawn noisily upon one another, concentric
and revolving, moving and inching back into itself. It was something I recognized
in myself, but the little differences were new and felt like hope. So I said it
when I thought nobody was listening. It burned my throat, but try as I might,
I couldn't un-speak it. I realized then that my orange draws down to peach
in the moments before it ignites the sunset; it burns like the countryside leaves
I had watched from the backseat of our family car when I was a child; it flares up,
mapping and coursing its way through evening's purple smoke like neon veins
in the darkness; it rests its head across my stomach and won't wash off my hands
in the moonlight; my orange breathes somewhere between the cuckolding snow
and the lust rattling beneath the robes of curious women who don't wear makeup;
my orange is the purple and brown tear stains on my shirt that fell by proxy as red
wine to mark both sorrow and joy; my orange will follow the ghost of Persephone
home as she endlessly oscillates between the Village and Alphabet City;
my orange blares from a gramophone and hits my ears as blue.

LUNCH

I know not to judge.

I also know I'm sitting at a small table
with an ornamental cup of Turkish coffee
listening to another conversation
about the weather. But it can't be possible.

I came here for revelations
in the eastern carpets, for the clink
of porcelain and the long, rhythmic
thuds of the waitress walking back
and forth. And because the coffee
tastes like salvation.

The next table isn't much better—the traffic
in Norway. It must be interesting. It's Norway,
after all. I wonder if Norway has dandelions,
and, if so, do pear-shaped men like me
obsess with poisoning every last one
in their yards?

I know not to judge.

But I am left with road signs, the weather,
and the horror of playing God between flowers
and weeds.

The silky bitterness in my mouth is worse
than redundant. It's my sole possession.

AFTERNOON AMONG RUINS

She was right,
sensibility is, at once, such a strange
and forgotten word
we scarcely know it's there.

It dangles above our conversations,
misused like an old cliché.
We treat it like experience
and never define it good or bad.

She was upright now,
her bare feet swinging back and forth
with some made-up-name of a color
from yester-week's impulse.

"You never pine away, not that you should."
These things I cannot change
I remind myself, and rhyme in my head
to push temptation away.

"My thoughts are
most beautiful when they just slip away,"
she continues, laying on the floor,
tucking her feet beneath her.

"If, in fact, beauty comes
from forgetfulness, when my skin curdles,
I will have lost my youth three times over,
yet you will remain remembered and young."

I remain as I was, at the window,
and don't turn around to meet her stare.
She seems so much more present,
so better suited to liberty when I look away.

The afternoon sun shifts slowly.
At least it finds courtesy in occasion,

even if we cannot.
But she'd no trouble with me looking her off.

Here, with the world spread before me
I am finally free from the shackles
of her great art, that subtle,
sexual epistemology.

I laugh in spite of my guilt.
My senses are not the substitute I had supposed,
and I find my way into my own place,
chuckling low and hearty at my thoughts:

My lips are most beautiful
when they're forgotten and free,
and wander places off my face
where eyes they cannot see.

WINTER

slippery
that's all
it ever was
never more
never less
it's as narrow
as it feels
and as vast
as it looks
no identity
crisis this time
a reminder
that changing
happens unless
stagnation
and slumber
forget to share
the vacancy
their hold
is the icy knife
upon the skin
the endless gray
the bone rattle
refusing to let go

THE DAY AND AFTER

When I started exploring empty hospital hallways
alone, walking past administration offices with rippled
glass windows and no lights inside, I knew something
had changed. Death was coming with a matter-of-fact
crawl. It was the same trick Inevitability uses to toy with grief
and turn hope into a helpless spectator. And later, my brothers
and I, spectators ourselves, with the monitors and machines
off so we'd stop searching for miracles among the numbers
and lights, placed our hands on our father's sleeping body
as he took his last breaths to join the wife he'd mourned
for a quarter century, the blue-eyed woman whose hand
he'd hold on walks after twenty-seven years of marriage,
still exchanging playful looks, too caught up to notice
if anyone else was watching.

The next night, my face weightless and my fingers numb
under the enormity of life that becomes clear when it's over, I
pulled into our driveway, the kids asleep in back, my wife
tired. A buck, a tall and slender six-point, stood up from where
he lay in the far corner of the yard near a young willow. A doe
rose up next to him. They stared when the van doors opened,
the buck taking two cautious steps forward as our shadows moved
one at a time back into our lives. But the doe bent down to eat
and shook her coat off in the damp air. She was at ease, as if
she knew something about the place her worried partner
did not. When the kids were inside, I went out alone to see them
again, but they were gone, the big yard emptier than usual.
They had slipped away, back into the night, together still,
or at last.

CONFIDENTIAL

When you are
beautiful

you never are
naked.

PHOTOSYNTHESIS

His feet, at least,
defy gravity.

Blue veins
and morning
disappear

in leather straps.
Rhinestones
for evocation,

for a sense of the past,
for seed.
A touch from the sky.

He feels both other
and himself, like a birth
he never had.

INGRID

When we were ruinous and guilty,
Undertakers of tranquility, the mouths of discontent,
The shattered, golden idol, Ingrid on the ledge,
Said mournfully sitting in her kitchen nook,
The morning sun lying about the room,
As she looked out the small window, to nobody at all,
That there is nothing more wasteful
Than a heart breaking on a lovely day.
"What darkness do I have to manufacture,"
She asked, "to hide something in this light?"

WE MET IN WINTER

and together grew
like weeds, uninhibited
by the ice and rain.
We pushed our way past
concrete, wild seeds
we are. We drank
from each other
and dared the sun into hiding.
We curled and plunged
our tongues into the detritus
that we had used for food
the many years before
our roots locked. Spring
made us unruly and
our dangling limbs overtook
the yard and then
the city, until we grew
over the face of time and
covered its eyes. We taunted
it and asked what it knows
of love. We called it a poor
gardener and said
it knows nothing
of autogenesis. That its
photosynthesis was
an idea that started
with the sun, but it didn't matter
because it acted as neither
a constraint nor catalyst
on us.

BARGAINING

Prelude (at dinner alone)

The pretty man is pretty, in deed.

The pretty lady is pretty, in deed.

Together, I know,
I know they are prettier still.

I think I've known their gravity.

But I cannot rise to greet it now.

Deeds so pretty in light.

I am full of unhelpful fragments tonight.

Part I (fall)

Venetian blinds in rear windows

Fall smiled back at us from behind its mask
and wore its confusion like a taunt.
It disguised the squirrels as bears in dry leaves
and seemed to conceal, at least for a while,
the awful onset of death and decay.
The sapling out front began to grow brown,
grew brittle before it grew up and slept.
Its youthful curl became fetal and small,

turned craggy, wrinkled, and was hauled away.
It slipped past summer on a back of gold,
and dressed the clouds in ubiquitous gray.
On windy days the bare limbs sounded like
an army advancing from all sides at once.
The shaking, cracking leaves made up new words

beneath the soft soles of our blue-light boots
declaring in tongues that "dying is birth."

The detergent smell of department stores
where in a cavern of track lights we shopped
for rulers, binders, and pens that we would
get in trouble for losing. Mom and Dad
lectured us about this and that
and the list of things we ought not do.
Reproaches, warnings, and perhaps some toys
to keep our childhood just a bit longer,
while the fields and sky turned opposite shades
of sameness. Repressed hues ran through our days,
as colors boiled from hand-me-downs
bled awake like the garden at midnight.
The streets held fewer cars and the ones that passed
did so bravely, one at a time. Even
lines of traffic seemed lonely at night when
night fell four hours earlier than in June.

These were the preludes to experience,
the soft underbellies of laconic dreams
that traced patterns, which Mom and Dad
daily assured the other were transient.

Venetian blinds and brothers' love

We waged a tomato war one night when
Mom and Dad went out to have dinner without us.
We whipped rotting fruit through the air,
pulled from the crates next to the garage,
around the corners of barns, the tiny blinking house,
at shadows and unsuspecting tufts
of tangled hair. The senseless, patient fruit
arched red and brown through the purple sky
—decomposed shooting stars in the night.

But then I picked up a small green one, hard
as a baseball, and caught my brother's ear
as he crouched down by the lilac branches
that reached out for him like crooked fingers
in the dark. I was old enough to fear
retaliation, but too young
to remember what happened next.

The scent of dry leaves—
best described as the scent
of dry leaves—the fallen life,
submitted to the never-ending reels
that flashed along with the projector's hand
bringing out the fruit mashed red in our hair,
and the years that our little feet covered
over the roots and long grass as we ran.

Endings were beginning all around us,
behind the yellow curtain of leaves
and in the blacksmith hammer of our rooms
where distance made everything large and small
and then large, again. Frame by frame,
it all came to focus. We grew up
in a slow-motion tremble. School started.
The new education of sizing up
strange boys and watching girls,
hoping they watched back.

We held dreams of firsts close to our ribs,
burrowing small shelters, squeezing
hope so tight we could not control it
and, for reasons not yet clear,
            hoped for more.

These memories creep their way
in pricks across the skin. They twist
and dive, shrink and grow.

They change with need.

Venetian blinds and lovers' songs

Making love with my fingers to the land,
pulling up tall grass by the handfuls,
cascading over the ebbing nighttime,
as if those sheaths and blades had cut
a straight line through the fences of the years,
bringing me dearer to the thought-dreams
where the ceiling fan washed over us both—
the silence of the beach in morning,
not far from the muffled furnaces that gasped
at the endless cerebral motion
of the water waiting for lovers' songs.

In the ruins of my shattered room,
figments, ligaments, and shadows,
pale and growing thin in broken circles,
trail images back and forth.

We watch two different movies
before us on the same screen.
We see nothing but the backs
of our own eyes.

In the pulsating projector light against my neck and hair,
I write down other people's words between each flash,
trace the figures on the screen, and
draw stolen pieces of time to life
from the movies of shadows and orange.

Venetian blinds and the Son of God

Lights go down. My anticipation
is still. My skepticism rises.
Images explode.

It's an adolescent show of noise,
a horrible series of lights that come
and go with no revelation.

Deus ex machina.
Reus ex machina.

I swear I saw Boo Radley
round the garage, his thick legs
swinging as he stepped into his throw.

I swear I saw some shadow
walk across the autumn yard
as rotten fruit arched and drove
its way through the darkness.

Some blight darkened the spaces
between the older and younger boys
as wounded summer crawled past one last time
and lay prostrate in the leaves.

Some specter masked in time-yet-spent
came to us before its appointed hour
and haughtily mocked our used-to-be.

Suddenly it was Bogart and Mother
dressed for the desert, nighttime heat,
and, though I don't know how I knew,
I knew she was dressed in blue.

And then there's me,
confused and opening a motel door
to drink tea with Tony Perkins.

Venetian blinds and confession

I do not want to read

I want to write

I do not want to watch this movie
I want to play a scene with you

No special observation to give
dusty in the sun
muddy in the rain
ordinary, just the ordinary

I do not want to observe any more
I want to feel you move in time

I no longer wish to think of the sun
I want my eyes closed under yours

I see no deeper than your downy arm hair,
brown and highlighted in the day,
your legs swinging as you walk—
the obvious, only the obvious

A cracked teacup and mine
A cracked teacup and Venetian blinds

Interlude (salt and denial)

Father told me,
his voice trembling
with the stiff, halting stammer
that had become
his substitute
for anger, that I
was to stay away and leave
those poor people
alone.

Scrape the driveway,
don't waste the salt,
kick the snow
off my boots
outside,
and put the bricks away
like I was told.

But, most important,
I was to leave those people alone.

And make sure I didn't waste the salt.

Part II (winter)

On the coldest nights of the year
winter undressed for me,
her front turned slightly
away, walking the yard,

as if I wasn't there, in shadows
of flake white mixed
with Prussian blue. The pale
January moon reflected

off her blanket. Dropping her chin,
she told me with a sort of impish
derision that idolatry is vulgar,
so I must paint her from memory.

She curled through my days
in powdery wisps of bleached ivy,
unadorned and penetrated
by the world.

When it was her turn,

she constricted, pulling tighter and tighter
until the land was blank.

Everything was new for a while.

By degrees, she became
my senseless logician, systematically
removing one variable
at a time. After the porch lights

came down, color was stuffed
into cardboard boxes for the season.
She left an occasional blue sky,
but made it so clear and cold

the chimney smoke struggled
to breathe. She reclined, brash and naked,
uninvited, but not refused—
un-annealed, not yielding.

In a room of manufactured heat, my
imagination pulled away her wrapping
with a slender brush to set her
in a grove of pines.

Her hips played against the manmade
colors, and her shadow twisted
like the face of God dancing for the lost,
seductive in their pointed ambiguity.

She shortened the days, erased
my footprints, and turned the dead
into ghosts who flailed anonymously
to stand out against her white.

The night wind drove snow
against my windows in tiny crunches

that sounded like my brush
bending upon the pocked
and porous canvas. It was the outside
coming in—winter breaking
her silence
with violent, persistent whispers.

I never had let the paint run my skin.
But after hours of clearing the walks,
when the feeling came back,
I let the tufts of bristling camel hair
circle the dry ends of my fingertips.
I painted my own hands
that had not seen sun in weeks and were
quite nearly as pale as the ground. My nerves
and blood were indistinguishable. A numbing
electricity surged from my arm to my chest
as those tangled, coarse ends drove away
the frightened admonishments
of waste that rested like stubborn marbles
in my ears. I removed my clothes,
and stood with my pale skin and the unshapely
fat of my inner thighs before a cracked mirror.

I painted from my roots
to the ends of my limbs.

I never knew the places the paint covered
still breathed instead of being suffocated.

I never knew a flash of life
blended with a trace of death
whenever colors are mixed.

Or that joy comes in shades so subtle
it circles back on itself to mimic emptiness.

Or that the smallest brush stroke
can make the skin jump and spark through the darkness.

Or that the tiniest ember torches the world,
but doesn't harm a soul.

But I know among them my blood burns hottest,
melting glaciers, not stopping
until the molting land and snow mix.

The smell of pine needles travels forwards and backwards at the same time.
The smell of pine needles seems to linger for days, but it's only minutes.
The smell of pine needs makes purple in the springtime and black in the summer.
The smell of pine needles makes memory remember that memories aren't always so.
The smell of pine needles has never been painted and never will.

The smell of the paint makes hearts leap from their chests
as it rises on low frequencies and clings to the floor,
as it floats and twists like rivulets of smoke along the floor,
and snakes its way into the senses of the brush hairs hovering just above the floor.
The brush changes everything and waltzes in middle of the floor,
and pushes and pulls the paint, dribbles and slides the paint back and forth on the floor.

Let me be the paint.
I will intoxicate the senseless passerby.

My blood can paint a sunset
to chase the red embarrassed off a rose.

I will dribble and splash through the air.

I will not worry about wasting one drop.

I will shower the world,
sending shivers down the spines
of the frugal and good.

I will spread myself over the frozen land,
curl and clump and be as layered as the earth.
I will warm it as it lie beneath me.

My seeds will penetrate their shells,
and I will water them as I twist and slide,
my edges balling up and my middle growing thin.

By God, I will give the painter a spring,
such a spring as has never been seen.

By God, I will bring warmth to the land,
a warmth that has yet to be formed.

By my hand I will turn back the death
from the earth and bring the cold to life.

And when winter returns to undress herself,
as we circle past the sun once more,
she will know she must lie beneath me
as the days grow long and the earth tilts my way.

Interlude (circles and complicated grief)

The days grew longer, and Persephone crept away unnoticed, walking in small steps across my yard, drawing a wide circle around the flower beds, never looking at me, shaking the mud and worms from the ends of her hair.

For a moment I did not know it was her. I had to look twice to be sure. I had to look twice to be sure. She shuffled through the grass leaving no trace she was there. When her shadow slipped past the barn, I was not sure if it had been her shawl, or the slow-waltzing leaves leftover from fall. I had to look twice to be sure. I thought I heard beneath her robes the soft clink of a chain, but it must have been the breeze playing the old weathervane.

Still I couldn't be sure, but when she paced back and forth weeping, I knew it was her. I put down my shovel when she walked backwards, creeping. It was too late. An image from the past sent her weeping.

Part III (spring)

PLANTING CATS

He inhaled a deep halting breath, like a large truck lurching to a stop. The glue smell radiated through his sagging cheeks to the barbed whiskers on his neck. On warm days it felt cold. But with the rain drizzling outside, and his wet work jacket heavy on his shoulders, it warmed him.

He ran a finger over the knife edge, examined it from every angle, and rummaged an old drawer for new blades. His hand trembled as tarnished brackets and bent nails slid and clanked together. He steadied himself on the work bench's splintered edge and flicked a door hinge aside as if that act of annoyance would itself cause a new razor to appear from the clutter.

The dull blade pulled at the small piece of carpet making a rough edge. Nobody would notice. He pulled out an old pair of carpet sheers and trimmed the loose threads, even though the animal could no longer bat at them.

He couldn't have brought the cat upstairs where it was warm. It was covered in its own piss. The vet cost money. He couldn't kill it himself. So he set it at the bottom of the stairs to look up at the kitchen table where it had once waited nightly for scraps.

It lay crumpled in its own filth and stench at the bottom of the basement stairs. For years it was overweight. Then for weeks, it was a urine-soaked skeleton, shivering and weakly moving its mouth, unable to mew. He had knelt down on the concrete floor and held out his hand. It pulled up its weaving head, lay it in his outstretched palm, and closed its eyes. No more shaking, no more fitful breaths. Two-thirds of its weight gone, the black fur matted and gnarled. It had looked fake, like a run over toy. Its yellow eyes no longer flashed like huge, unblinking marbles. He stayed there for a long moment, feeling the life drain from the house. Then he gently put the animal's small head down, letting it rest on the bed of old clothes, and he sat with it for a while.

The low rush of the furnace seemed correct. Cause and effect made sense, so did life and death. The simplicity of the moment made up for its loneliness.

The shovel breaking the wet ground sounded like muffled glass. Pale, cut worms twisted against the invisible lines of the hole. Rain beaded along the brim of his hat and glue balled up on his rough skin.

A carpet-lined box and shade tree were his penance for never liking the animal. It never came when he called, required food, but gave no comfort, and stared at him from across the room. Even before it died, it was a thing from the past. Since he no longer thought of the past, it was something he didn't understand.

He put an old picture of the cat sitting on his wife's lap in the box.

The cat itself was a photograph of sorts, some black and white snapshot from the past that had crawled out of its frame—unruly, misshapen, difficult thing. It wasn't like a cat at all. It was a glassy ornament that snapped at him with its inattention. It bit and lashed out at his poverty and rough hands—spiteful thing. Good to be dead.

Later, after dinner, when the house was big, when the silence stared at him like a cold cat from across the room, unimpressed with his small dinner or the voices from the television, when evening clawed away at him like an old cat that didn't want to be bothered, when he heard a noise that he thought was the cat, when a brush of air passed signifying movement, he never once looked around. In the night when empty came to life, it had no one about the house to which to speak, nobody to make eye contact with or play a hand of cards. The past exists only in relation to what comes after it. The cat could not haunt him if he never regarded it as having been alive.

He put away the brown bag full of photos from where he had retrieved the buried picture. He reckoned they were illusions.

If time stands still it could never have been time to begin with. So an image of time stopped was a lie. Photographs were thieves, a mockery of moving moments robbed of their identity—stolen bits of light waiting to be executed, staring like an old cat with yellow eyes that oscillate between curiosity and contempt—predator and prey, reminder and remainder in one. The snap and slide of a brown paper bag. The opening and closing of an attic door. A thoughtless thump.

As he lay in bed that night, the pictures in the attic pulled at him and began to form a movie in his mind. Light.Color. Contrast.Tone.Line.Form.Pattern. Balance. Tomorrow would be a clear day for planting flowers, instead of cats. He pulled his blanket tight against his chin and pictured a camera with a cat's eye for a flash. Evil tool.

He thought for a moment of prayer, but God was a picture—a pattern of light or a series of lines, which changed depending on his mood, something that existed in a drawer someplace else. God was stolen from eternity and frozen—like old wedding photos filtered through some senseless lens that knew enough to allow light, but could not know what it was recording.

Exposure.Texture.Depth.Movement. Death was a picture.

That cat named God stared at him from across the bedroom, always unhelpful. That photograph called God resembled himself, lonely and meticulously ordering his world. Like God, he kept all of his conflicting feelings at the surface so that when he eventually chose the one that best fit his surroundings, he could pretend it was, and had been, his truth.

He had always loved the cat he said softly, his voice breaking a little from not being used, as he pulled the covers to his chin and slept.

Interlude (acceptance)

First lips, then eyes. You must remove your chin.
Pull out your hair. The grass will replace it.
Remove your clothes, but begin with the sleeves.
The dust you breathe is the skin of the dead.

It always has been, and yet you have lived.
Yes, flesh, too. You are just an animal,
caught in the headlights while crossing the road.
Now give me your feet, then up to your knee.
Keep moving up. More. More. You'll not need those.
Once the arms go it's a dream and it's done.
Patient, not so much has changed as you think,
just long division and the same walls each day.
Stand straight. Stand tall. Live a life of angles.
Now cut them flat, set them on fire, and dance.
Dance circles around them, but don't get caught.
Why won't you move? How dare you disobey?
There was no sound for you to turn your head,
no whisper, no words, at least not for you.
Your pieces scattered and naked are gone
and are for others now. You cannot hide.
Save yourself. Do not cower. You must live.
All things pass. The secret
                                        is nothing dies.

Part IV (summer)

Summer is when youth plays, but is not for youth.

It is proof the good crop was fertilized with lost seeds, proof no death has
ever stopped the world, proof of a good god, a toddler god, and no god at
all, proof of execution, proof the executioner can show his face without
shame.

Summer is to be close to life, and to be close to life is to grow from
the decomposition while running towards it.

Summer is the season of toil, of sin and redemption, lust for lushness.

Summer is muscular arms, taught legs, the bucking and kicking of skin
until birth marks are gone.

Summer is for the laborer, composer, hammer, blister, migrant, body exploding in the light, scorched skin, hurt backs, blood clotted with dirt, seminal fluid, hips pointed to the sky, street kids looking for the divine. Machines and gadgets have not changed this.

Summer is proof that voices reach back in a vacuum when there is nothing left to say in the present.

Proof the speed of sound is slower than the will to bury.

Proof echoes are a delusion, a bending of reality forced on the senses.

Proof that thunder and silence lie on their backs with serrated claws flailing aimlessly at the stillness of our bedrooms.

Proof everything that exists in the light still exists in the dark.

Proof of willful blindness.

Proof celebration forgets and proof it must.

Proof the rain has its own appetite and flicks its tongue to taste the edges of our skin and drink our dangling sweat.

Proof poetry is the compressed undercurrent working its way through our blood that cannot be distilled by the liver.

Proof that the people drinking beneath their private shade trees haven't unzipped their own necks and backs with a straw in hand to see if their spinal fluid tastes like nectarines, vodka, Sundays, death, or wine;

Proof they haven't walked through Willie McTell at midnight with counterfeit-suicide imposters, discussing segregationist books where the black text is ripped screaming and wriggling from the white page, playing jug-band ukuleles for Desdemonas in drag that skip down small-town streets, lifting their knees to their elbows trying to leap to Heaven in one step;

Proof they haven't plucked instrumental rags from cascading trumpets of jazz players in front of the warm echo of hazel-wood fires that fill their lungs with hot and the comprehension of their own names;

Proof they've never known the warm, dappled grass that grows in the golden stitches of unzipped jeans after watching the morning birds for three days straight without sleep;

Proof they've never stared into a mirror with the cracked face of Hester Prynne and that wild devil dancing on her arm, convinced they were the only man who had the right to love her forever;

Proof they've never walked the sweaty streets with Wakefield by an oil lamp at 3:00 a.m. passing themselves in the dim light for a chance to run their fingers down their own faces with twenty years between themselves;

Or straddled the bridge from Paterson to Innisfree with wristwatches that lie to them about their parents' metamorphosis;

Proof they've never gone antiquing in search of the perfect silver coffee spoon from which to taste the black hale that trembles from their eyeballs as they choke on the pears and apples from the all-night ferry;

Proof they've never known Boo Radley as an aching shadow, a halo of wild hair, cracked paint, and small patterns pulled away with time, a tattered shirt that would not look near so tattered in color, wandering the bleached and sweaty streets of America's Imbeciles' Row;

Proof they don't require proximity to the combustible dynamo that straddles existence and extinction, that holy trinity of self, birth, and commas.

Summer is supposed to be where the effort of life goes into becoming, a journey towards harvest along a continuum of days that stretches out from dawn's rosy red fingers to evening's purple clouds.

Purple is the blues with a drop of blood. It's in the lilacs, irises, and sunset.

It's the color lymphedema turned your skin as cancer grew through you.

It was spring, but it was the summer of your life. You never got autumn. Your orange would have been beautiful.

There is so much I never will know about you. I have allowed those things their own life.

There is so much I don't remember.

I remember you weren't ready to die.

Every ending is the fact of two beginnings.

But endings and beginning are alive. They breathe, speak, and learn how to grow. They don't require acknowledgment. They certainly don't need light.

The past is a tattoo, not a shadow. It does not wait for time that has not been allocated to a purpose. It shows itself in the midst of the commotion. It is most pronounced in times of change.

Calendars and clocks fool us into believing that life is a straight line.

Nothing gets buried for long.

The past is a poor guest. It does not respect memory.

Charles David James Case is a poet and novelist living in East Aurora, New York, just south of Buffalo, with his wife, five daughters, murderous cat, and neurotic spotted dog.

Charles holds a B.A. in philosophy and a Juris Doctor. He has jumped on stage with Bob Dylan.

In 2014, despite having made partner, he left the full-time practice of law to write and raise his young family.

Charles grew up as the youngest of four boys in Newark, New York, a small town on the Erie Canal between Rochester and Syracuse. Even though they lived on a budget that often fell short of a shoestring, his parents gave themselves to their sons and community. Until classmates made fun of his at-home haircuts and second-to-third-hand clothes, Charles had believed they were rich. He was right.

Charles is a jazz fan (because the self-imposed exile of writing doesn't isolate a person nearly enough these days), hiker, cyclist, and rather bad living-room guitar player. He believes in wandering with the purpose of wandering more as a sort of religion. He hopes to spend his life searching for his favorite poem, book, or song and never find them.

CPSIA information can be obtained
at www.ICGtesting.com
Printed in the USA
BVHW08s1308260818
525256BV00003B/86/P